Anonymous

A Comparative View of the Public Burdens of Great Britain and Ireland

Anonymous

A Comparative View of the Public Burdens of Great Britain and Ireland

ISBN/EAN: 9783744724302

Printed in Europe, USA, Canada, Australia, Japan

Cover: Foto ©ninafisch / pixelio.de

More available books at **www.hansebooks.com**

A

COMPARATIVE VIEW

OF THE

PUBLIC BURDENS

OF

GREAT BRITAIN

AND

IRELAND.

WITH

A PROPOSAL for putting both ISLANDS on an
EQUALITY, in Regard to the FREEDOM of
FOREIGN TRADE.

Omnino, qui reipublicæ præfuturi sunt, duo Platonis præcepta
teneant; unum ut utilitatem civium sic tueantur, ut quæcunque
agunt ad eam referant, obliti commodorum suorum; alte-
rum ut totum corpus Reipublicæ curent, ne dum partem ali-
quam tueantur, reliquas deserant.

Cic. de Offic.

LONDON:

PRINTED, AND

DUBLIN:

Reprinted by R. BURTON, (No. 3) CAPEL-STREET,
MDCCLXXIX.

A

COMPARATIVE VIEW

OF THE

PUBLIC BURDENS

OF

GREAT BRITAIN and IRELAND, &c.

THOUGH the inhabitants of Great Britain and Ireland are fo ftrongly connected by the natural fituation of their territory, by intermarriages, by an intermixture of property, by a conformity of laws and interefts, and by many other ties; yet the narrow policy of former ages has raifed up a wall of feparation between them, that has hitherto greatly obftructed their mutual profperity. We are every day made to confider Canada and Florida as one territory, though they are more remote from each other than Copenhagen is from Gibraltar; and yet we abfurdly look upon Great Britain and Ireland as ftates having different interefts, though the diftance between their fhores in fome places is not fo great as that between the oppofite fhores of feveral friths

in this island. — Were the shores of Lake Erie
or Lake Superior, in North America, to be
well peopled with British subjects, we should
regard it as the height of impolicy if the
mercantile intercourse between the northern
and southern shores of the same lake were
to be checked by high duties and prohibitions. Those lakes however, are much more
confiderable bodies of water, than the channel that feparates the shores of Great Britain
and Ireland, which channel, in true policy,
ought always to have been confidered but as
a mere arm of the fea, giving us the advantage of a more extended fea coaft, and faci-
litating the conveyance of merchandize by
coafting navigation.

Exclufive privileges neverthelefs having
been once introduced, from the weak principle of drawing the chief refources of government from exported and imported merchandize;* each island foon began to believe
the other poffeffed of fuch advantages, as
rendered prohibitions neceffary for the fecu-
rity of their refpective interefts. This def-
tructive fyftem is now thought by many
people to be the natural fyftem; or at leaft
they alledge, that the public burdens borne
by the fubjects in each island are fo difpro-
portionate as to render a commercial equality for both extremely difficult, if not impracticable. Others, with much more reafon, regard the reciprocal reftraints on trade
between the two iflands as moft unnatural;
and think that it would be far from being
difficult or impracticable to adjuft the differences

* A fund of taxation at that time probably not one tenth part fo
large as that of the produce of the land, joined to the internal confumption.

ferences in the public burdens of each, were
an accurate examination and eftimate of thofe
differences but once obtained. I have, in the
following pages, attempted fuch an examination and fuch an eftimate, with a view to the
eftablifhment of an equality of trade in both
iflands, hoping for the indulgence of the
public, if, upon a fubject of fuch national importance, which has not hitherto been made
an object of difcuffion by any of our political
or commercial writers that I have met with,
I fhould not be able to give all the fatisfaction
that could be wifhed. When the fubject
once comes under the deliberation of the parliament of each kingdom, the happy confequences flowing from an equality of trade in
both iflands, will then appear with all their
evidence and force, and we fhall have reafon to be aftonifhed, how fuch an eftablifhment, fo cafily to be accomplifhed, and now
become fo neceffary, could have been fo long
neglected.

By the prefent commercial fyftem, Ireland
confiders herfelf as the moft aggrieved; but
fhe has been long accuftomed to complain of
other hardfhips than that of a limited trade,
which hardfhips, when the actual fituation of
that ifland is examined, will appear to be
founded more on popular opinion than rea-
lity. The moft plaufible of thefe is, the ex-
ceffive drain of wealth occafioned by the
abfentees or landholders not refident in Ireland, which the Irifh allege as a grievance
peculiar to them; and the next is the great
weight of their taxes paid directly to government. Now, though I acknowledge, that
the burdens and grievances of Ireland are
very confiderable, and, on our fide, in the
higheft

highest degree impolitic, I hope neverthelefs
to make it evident, that the number of her
abfentees, and the excefs of her taxes cannot be reckoned among thofe grievances‡.
I deny that the drain of abfentees is a tax
peculiar to Ireland. It is a tax which the capital of every great empire draws from all its
remote provinces, and in the Britifh ftate is
not more paid by Ireland than by the diftant
counties in Great Britain. This will appear evident to the conviction of every reader, who confiders the nature of the internal circulation of a ftate, and examines
what are the chief fources of its opulence and
wealth.

The country is the chief productive fund
of national wealth; and though it be continually pouring into the capital city, yet
the fmall ftock that remains behind, added
to the frugality that prevails there, fuffices,
with the bounty of nature, to afford new
fupplies, and at the fame time to maintain a
kind of eafinefs in the remote towns and
villages, provided the demands of the capital be not exorbitant. An hundred men employed in country labour will produce more
to the ftate, than an hundred thoufand livery
fervants, coachmen, and chairmen in London; for thefe laft, though not employed in
deftroying and flaughtering, produce no more
national wealth than an hundred thoufand

‡ The people of Ireland think their circumftances much worfe than
they really are, and have had many pfeudo patriots among them, the
foremoft of whom is the witty author, but wretched politician, Swift,
who have ftudioufly endeavoured to make them believe fo. For one
monument in memory of Swift as a politician, the Irifh ought to erect
twenty to the memory of bifhop Berkeley, as there is much more true
political knowledge in his Queries alone, than in all Swift's works put
together.

foldiers

soldiers encamped on the same spot would produce. London, so far from enriching the country, is in great part maintained and supported by the distant provinces gratis. For example, suppose the rents of the absentees from the county of Northumberland, which probably exceed fifty thousand pounds, are to be paid at the capital, and that a company of merchants at Newcastle send coals to that value to London, those merchants may be paid for their coals by bills of exchange upon the stewards of the absentees of the same county, in which case it is plain, Northumberland not only furnishes the coals, but furnishes the payment of them. Again, supposing a Lincolnshire grazier brings up a thousand head of cattle to London; the butcher who purchases those cattle, we shall suppose for eight thousand pounds, by paying that sum into the treasury, may procure from thence a draught of the same value upon a collector of the excise in Lincolnshire, which he gives to the grazier, who receives cash for it upon his return home. I know not whether this precise method be used in this kingdom; but I know that it is practised in France; and whatever be the channel of exchanges, it comes in the end to the same thing, and plainly proves that Lincolnshire pays Lincolnshire, 'and London receives the cattle for nothing. These examples may suffice in place of an hundred others; and may serve to check the presumption of the Londoners, who vaunt the prodigious supplies that city affords the state, and expect that their factious deliberations should have a controling influence in national counsels.

But

But if the diftant provinces be continually pouring into the capital more than ever returns, what becomes of all that wealth centering in London? That queftion may be anfwered by another; what becomes of all the coals carried to London? Both are confumed there. If all the demands of the rich landholders, abfentees from their eftates by their refidence in London, added to the demands of government upon the diftant provinces were to be paid in cafh, it is plain that within the compafs of one year, not five fhillings in filver would be found in Great Britain out of the county of Middlefex. But both the wants of the ftate and of the rich proprietors require a circulation of a different kind. The taxes and rents are moftly exchanged on the fpot for provifions and merchandife, neceffaries wanted at the capital, and the bills for thofe provifions and merchandife ballance the country's debts to the center of government and chief refidence of the land proprietors, the money or cafh, both in town and country, remaining at its ufual equilibrium, unlefs fome extraordinary demand of government, fuch as the maintenance of an army abroad, fhould draw a more than ordinary proportion of it to the capital, in order to be tranfported out of the kingdom. Ireland, therefore, cannot ftate the expences of its abfentees as a peculiar hardfhip, for in that article, it has only neighbour's fare, it being certain that the remote provinces, both within and without the ifland of Great Britain, receive no equivalent whatever for great part of what they furnifh to the capital, except the equivalent of protection and defence. At the capital refides
the

the intelligence that directs government, accompanied by many luxurious appendages, together with ten thousands of idlers, allured thither by pleasure only, with great numbers more, whose occupations have no relation to industry, and all are consumers, yielding no retribution of wealth for wealth. Those in the country, on the other hand, who give themselves to agriculture, are always employed in producing something that did not exist before; and this produce, on the whole, in every well regulated state, ought to be so abundant as amply to suffice for the maintenance, the clothing, housing firing, &c. of the whole inhabitants, with some reserve for an accumulation of wealth. Bodies politic, in this respect, have an apt resemblance to the animal body, and with them every day verifies the truth of the fable of the belly and the members, the latter feeding the former; but as this is a natural state, it is a state that does not require a remedy, and nothing but ignorance or cross humour can reckon it a disease.

The murmurers about the absentees from Ireland found their whole reasoning upon a sophism, never considering Ireland as a part of a great sovereignty; but falsely supposing it a free independent sovereignty of itself, maintaining itself in peace with its neighbours by its own strength, and regulating all its political and commercial interests freely by its own deliberations. But no man of sense and candour, the least acquainted with the subject, will affirm that to be the actual state of Ireland. The army maintained there, by the confession of the Irish themselves, is intended only for quelling the domestic dis-

turbances

turbances of the peace, and is allowed by thofe gentlemen of Ireland, who know their country well, not to be too numerous for that purpofe. Againft a foreign enemy, they have the protection of the fleet and army of Great Britain, joined with their own auxiliary force, and that of American Britons, all forming but one mafs of power, capable of making itfelf refpected by any ftate in Europe, that fhould think of annoying it. This formidable power muft have a center fomewhere; and this center is fituated moft commodioufly for the whole in Great Britain. What limits bodies politic ought to be reduced to, or what extent they ought to acquire, for the beft well-being of the people that compofe them, is a queftion that politicians and lawgivers will never be able to refolve. I reafon only upon the actual ftate of Great Britain and Ireland as forming one fovereignty, fwayed and directed by one fupreme deliberation, all the parts of which ought to contribute to the fupport of the whole. And Ireland, when confidered in this view, will be found to be more favoured in the article of abfentees, than many remote parts of England; for fince Dublin is become fo large, fo populous and elegant a city, with eftablifhed theatres, and abundance of other amufements for the affluent, nearly on a par with thofe of London, by far the greateft number of the nobility and gentry of Ireland, who do not refide upon their eftates, make that the field for difplaying their luxury, or for enjoying the pleafures of felect focieties and literary intimacies, all of which that capital affords in an eminent degree. The nobility and gentry of the nor-

thern

thern counties of England have no such gay and agreeable place of resort to prevent their flocking to London; and whithersoever they travel, their rents must follow them.

In a monarchical government, the very form of the constitution necessarily draws many of the nobility and gentry to the chief residence of the supreme governor. When the number of those absentees becomes excessive, I do not deny but it may be impoverishing to the provinces, and consequently prejudicial to the whole community. But Ireland is much more secure against such an evil than the remote provinces of Great Britain, for, as I have above observed, the elegancies and luxuries of Dublin, with the parliament resident there, will always serve as checks against the temptation of flocking to London, and will retain at home a proportional greater number of the Irish gentry, when compared with the gentry of Great Britain. Though in such a republican state as Switzerland, a large capital city composed of absentees, is not necessary, and would be extremely detrimental: yet in a commercial nation wholly surrounded by the sea, having a maritime city for the capital, and a naval force to maintain for its defence, the very resort of the landed gentlemen thither, provided it be not excessive, contributes to diffuse prosperity over the whole, by creating a great intercourse by sea between the seat of empire and the provinces, and inducing greater numbers of people to prosecute a sea-faring life. The immense coasting trade of Great Britain is owing to the vast concourse of people to London; and while this trade excites to industry in the remote parts in a greater degree than could be

expected

expected if every gentleman were to spend his rent among his tenants upon his estate, the cause that promotes it may be reckoned beneficial to the kingdom. The people in Ireland cannot justly allege that the counties in Great Britain can afford to pay large sums to absentees at London, better than Ireland can, since the British absentees reside in the same country and great part of the sums must return back by circulation. From the examples of Northumberland and Lincolnshire, it appears plain that the returns are not to be counted upon. This traffic is not so much a circulation as a *current* flowing one way, and ending in evaporation or consumption: but at the same time partly assisting in giving activity to the machine of government, upon which depends the security and prosperity of the whole.

From the above reasoning, with regard to the absentees, we may safely draw the following corollay, That the apprehensions of those are wholly groundless, who think that if Ireland were permitted a free liberty in trade and commerce, she would even drain the opulence from Great Britain, and soon become of more prejudice than service to us. It is demonstrably clear, that while the seat of government of the British nation remains in this island, Ireland, like every other distant member, must contribute her share to the luxurious waste at the capital, and consequently the superiority of wealth must always be on our side. In proportion as Ireland becomes richer, so will she prosper more within herself, and contribute more to the opulence of Great Britain. Besides, commerce, like every other thing, has its ne plus ultra, or fixt limit; for allowing that the low

rents

rents and low wages in Ireland might at firft
act as a premium in promoting its foreign
trade, and that by a large balance it foon
accumulated much wealth, yet that very
wealth, by enlarging the mafs in circulation,
would raife the price of land, and of every
thing elfe, and of courfe check the farther
enlargement of the trade, and leffen the annual ballance. We do not read in aneient
hiftory that the Romans, after they had an-
nexed Sicily to their empire, put the leaft
reftraint upon its trade, or thought that
ifland would fwallow up Italy. Nay, the fmall
kingdom of Naples has not the leaft jealoufy
of Sicily, though the proportion between
the infular and continental territory of the
Neapolitans is much greater than between
Ireland and Great Britain. There is a fafhion
in politics as in every thing elfe. Towards the
end of the laft century, and in the beginning
of this, the great opulence of the Dutch aftonifhed all their neighbours, and the political writers of thofe and of modern times,
having confidered their narrow territory, and
the various manufactures carried on by them,
have, very erroneoufly, attributed their
wealth to thofe two circumftances, the importance of which they have exaggerated beyond meafure. Now nothing is more eafily
demonftrable than that the Dutch have been
indebted for their power and opulence, not
to manufactures, but to territorial riches, and,
next to that, to the univerfal freightage of
the products and merchandize of other nations, added to their fpirit of frugality and
hoarding. The Dutch, I fancy, would have
been far from adopting the maxims attributed to them by our political writers; and if
they

they could have affociated to their republic four or five of the adjoining provinces, they would not have reftrained thofe provinces from pufhing their induftry and commerce as far as they poffibly could. The notion of concentering manufactures, where the territory is large and fertile, is in the higheft degree abfurd. A farmer who fhould lay all his dung, or throw all his feed into his garden, could not expect fuch return, as he who prudently diftributed both among the different inclofures of his farm.

If Ireland cannot count the number of her abfentees as a political grievance peculiar to her, neither can fhe reckon herfelf aggrieved by the excefs of taxes raifed for the direct fupport of government. Taxes in every ftate ought to bear a certain proportion to the wealth or yearly income of that ftate, and the proper ftandard for computing this wealth or income, though not the full and exact meafurement of it, is the yearly rents of all the lands, joined to the ballance of the foreign trade. The land-rents of Ireland are generally ftated, by thofe who are well acquainted with the country, at two millions five hundred thoufand pounds. Above forty years ago, two millions was reckoned an undervaluation for thofe rents, and many people now fuppofe them near three millions. A deduction of a confiderable part ought to be made on account of the abfentees; for it would not be juft to count that as a revenue, which goes out of the kingdom; yet as Ireland acquits herfelf of that debt, whatever it be, by the profits arifing from the ballance of her trade with Great Britain and other ftates, this laft may, in the
present

present computation, be put as an equivalent for the preceding deduction, especially as it is known to yield a surplus. We have then, as the standard of the actual wealth of Ireland, two millions five hundred thousand pounds†; and the taxes amount, communibus annis, to about eight hundred thousand pounds, which is not quite a third of the supposed fund.

Let us examine the burdens of Great Britain by the same standard. The amount of the land-tax in England makes the rents of the lands ten millions; but as that valuation is generally allowed to be hardly more than one half of the value, we shall state the real rents of all the lands of England at twenty millions. At the union of England and Scotland, the land rents of the latter, were most impolitically and absurdly rated but at a fortieth part of the lands of the former, which were then computed but at ten millions. The land-rents of Scotland by that estimation would only make two hundred and fifty thousand pounds; but as that was a great undervaluation, and very considerable improvements have been made there within these sixty years, it will be nearer the truth to reckon the land-rents of that part of the island, one million and an half, which added to the rents of England, makes the sum of twenty-one millions and an half. To this must be added the balance of our foreign trade, which is by some computed at three millions, by others

† I must caution my reader not to think this the whole fund, though it has been ignorantly taken as such by Swift. It is only a standard of wealth justly proportioned to that in Great Britain, and the original source of every other fund.

others at four, and by others at four and an
half. We shall take the highest sum, which
added to the land-rents, makes twenty-six
millions as the standard of taxation for Great
Britain. Let us now see what proportion
the taxes or public supplies bear to that fund.
The grants for the year 1770, every article
appropriated, amount to above seven millions; but to these must be added other taxes
upon the people, such as four millions five
hundred thousand pounds, for the annuities
yearly due to the public creditors; eight hundred thousand pounds as his majesty's civil list,
and at least seven hundred thousand pounds,
as the unappropriated surplus of the sinking
fund, all which added together, make a sum
of thirteen millions annually raised upon the
people of Great Britain, in time of profound
peace; and upon the fund above stated of
twenty-six millions. While Great Britain then
is paying about one half, Ireland is paying
not quite one third; or, in other words,
while the productive fund of Ireland stands
to that of Great Britain nearly as one to ten,
her public burdens, compared to those of this
island, are only as one to nineteen. If a trifling
part of the taxes of Ireland are sent out of the
kingdom, the taxes sent from this island to
foreign parts will be found to be twenty times
as great, and this is a burden which foreign
acquisitions, such as Minorca and Gibraltar,
entail upon Great Britain. But those acquisitions are judged necessary for maintaining
the rank which this nation at present holds
in Europe; and in supporting those charges,
and every other that may properly be called
foreign, Ireland pays but a very small share

in

in proportion to her income, and when considered as a collective part of the British nation.

I have avoided taking the quantity of money, in either kingdom into the account of
its respective productive funds, as that is
almost universally measured by the rents of
the lands, excepting in some commercial states,
where the spirit of amassing and hoarding in
a length of years forms many large dead
funds, which are not known to exist, but as
great occasions bring them into circulation.
Much money cannot long be used in circulation, without proportionably affecting the
rents of the lands; nor can the rents of lands
be heightened in any extraordinary degree,
without rendering a greater quantity of money, either nominal or real, necessary in
circulation. The practice of modern times
likewise, in the unlimited coinage of paper,
shews that it depends wholly upon the incli-
nation of a community, whether it should
have much money or not; and Ireland, if she
pleased, might in a few months possess as
full an abundance of money as Great Britain. If a large currency, or as M. Pinto
calls it, l'augmentation de numéraire, be so
essential as he represents it, Ireland would do
well directly to issue out a greater quantity
of paper; but I suspect, in that case, the augmented price of her products and manufactures would soon convince her, that she had
done better to have founded her politics
upon the maxim of Sir William Petty, " that
" it is very ill husbandry to increase the cash
" of a nation otherwise than by increasing
" its wealth, simul & semel." This maxim

C   likewise

likewife requires its modification; but we fee
in the example of our North American colonies, that focieties may yearly increafe their
wealth and opulence, without having any
money among them that can be faid to have
an intrinfic value. And Great Britain herfelf would foon be in the fame circumftances
. with her American colonies, with regard to
cafh, were fhe obliged directly to refund all
the money fhe at prefent owes to foreigners;
there is therefore no great reafon to look
upon the quantity of circulating money as
of much confequence in the eftimate of the
yearly income of a ftate.

It has been proved, I think demonftrative-
ly, that the taxes raifed in Ireland are nearly
one half lefs than thofe raifed in Great Britain, in proportion to the refpective ability
of each ifland. But fhould Ireland be put
upon an equality with Great Britain in point
of the freedom of trade, which true policy
dictates the propriety of, it is but natural to
require, that fhe fhould alfo be placed nearer
to an equality with this ifland in refpect to
the public burdens; and that may be done
moft advantageoufly for Ireland, by a land-
tax, to rife and fall, as the land-tax in Great
Britain rifes and falls; for in all military ar-
maments, there can be no caufe of expence
to this ifland, that ought not to be a propor-
tionable caufe of expence to the neighbouring
ifland. If no other civilized ftate in Europe
but Ireland, and none in Afia that we know
of, and no community among the European
colonies in America, think proper wholly to
exempt lands from public burdens, an im-
partial confiderer, without weighing any
other circumftances, would be apt to conclude
that there is more of impolicy than true policy

licy in fuch an exemption in Ireland. But
fhould he find that taxes in Ireland, inftead
of being laid upon the *moft opulent*, are, in
many cafes laid upon the *moft miferable*, who
have hardly any means of induftry, he would
think himfelf juftified in affirming, that the
nation could not thrive as might be expected, till a reform was made in fuch an effential
article. The lands in Ireland lie under a
heavier burden than if they were to pay three
fhillings, or even four fhillings, in the pound
to the fupport of government; which burden preffes alfo upon the commerce and induftry of the inhabitants. This burden is the
high rate of the intereft of money in that
ifland, the difadvantages of which are generally acknowledged, and need not here be
detailed; but, happily for Ireland, and I may
alfo fay for Great Britain, the legiflature
of that kingdom have it wholly in their
power, by the eafieft and moft conftitutional
means, to reduce that rate to three per
cent. Such a reduction of intereft would
of confequence raife the value of eftates
nine or ten years purchafe, that is, would
render land a poffeffion by one fourth more
valuable than at prefent; which would be
more than a full equivalent for a direct tranfi-
tion to a land-tax, a tax which, like all
others, is paid by the induftrious confumers.
Were the value of the lands of Ireland doubled, the gentlemen of that ifland would not
only be gainers, but the inhabitants would
find the taxes lefs burdenfome. Now almoft
the fame confequences would follow, if, inftead of the value of the lands, the quantity
of induftry were doubled, which I believe few
people acquainted with Ireland will deny to

be

be possible with the present number of hands. But the truest means to augment not only the marketable but the real value of lands, is to augment the stock of industry; and nothing so likely to effect that as the opening a free trade to Ireland, and the taking off and removing the oppressive burdens from the lower class of people, which they labour under from injudicious taxes, and I am afraid from discouraging leases.

The former of these depends upon the joint concurrence of the legislature of both kingdoms; but the latter may be effected by the parliament of Ireland singly, and is so essential to the prosperity of that island, that were the same restrictions upon its trade even still to be continued, a new plan of taxation ought nevertheless to be pursued, in order to excite the poor to industry, and check the propensity to expensive luxuries in people of small incomes, who instead of following business, are tempted, from the present indulgence of the legislature, to rank themselves among the unindustrious classes. Were the great commercial cities, such as Dublin, Cork, Waterford, Belfast, &c. but properly attentive to their own as well as to the national prosperity, they might be expected to sollicit such a reformation in the mode of taxation, which would give new life to commerce throughout the whole island. Where the poor have the means and the spirit of industry, they can bear great taxes, as their application to labour is a rich fund; but in a country where indolence and oppression keep the poor people beggarly, a very small imposition is more than they can bear, and makes them immediately desert their habitations, or shelter
themselves

themselves still more in idleness and misery, against vexations which they look upon as arbitrary. All means to animate them to industry ought to be used; and among the most effectual may be reckoned the exempting them, as much as possible, from all direct impositions to government, and granting them long leases upon moderate terms; and should trade be opened, the assurance of good and constant wages to the workman and manufacturer. What encouragements or discouragements poor farmers in Ireland meet with from their landlords, I cannot pretend to mention; but we have one very bad symptom, in regard to the protection and encouragement of agriculture, in the frequent advertisements for tenants that are to be met with in the Dublin news-papers.

The impositions of government upon the poor may be judged of more easily; but though these impositions in the mass should not be found to be very burdensome, yet, from their discouraging nature, they may check ten times their value in industry, and in that view are very impoverishing to the state. It is not a plan of thriving to pay a million to receive one hundred thousand pounds; but if all the non-working and half-working people in Ireland, were but to labour as the lower classes of people in England, they would add above a million annually to the national income, which would have the effect of making provisions and merchandize more abundant, or of lowering the prices of them considerably. The conclusion is not always just, that because rents and wages are low in a state, one may expect in that state an abundance of every thing at the cheapest prices.

prices. On fuch a fuppofition, Siberia would be the moft abundant country, where one may have twenty or thirty acres of the fineft meadow for the rent of one penny. The truly affluent country is that where, independent of the mafs of money in circulation, an abundance and variety of products are every day ready to be offered in exchange for an abundance and variety of manufactures, the whole the effect of the induftry of the inhabitants. The two great fources of national opulence are, the fertility of the foil and the labour of the poor; and when this laft is checked by injudicious taxes, and other difcouraging circumftances, it has the fame effect upon the mafs of the people as if the lands were rendered by fo many degrees more barren. One ought, therefore, to be as zealous in removing indolence from the people, as in removing barrennefs from the foil. The moft direct means for the former in Ireland, would be to punifh with the utmoft feverity ftrolling mendicants, who not only infeft the towns and villages, but parade in great numbers through the large opulent cities; to contrive premiums, if poffible, for the induftrious; and, by giving fome marks of diftinction to thofe who are well lodged and well clothed, to fill their minds with the fpirit of amaffing, which would foon make them tax each other, from rivalfhip, ten times more than they are now taxed by the ftate, and yet all increafe their own wealth at the fame time, and confequently the national wealth.

The eager defire of gaining and amaffing among individuals has the moft powerful of all effects in the promoting of induftry in

a com-a community. Suppose forty shoe-makers, in a town, agree to make only a certain number of pairs of shoes a week, and to sell their shoes at a high price, in order to enjoy every other day as a holiday; if any one of these shoe-makers breaks the agreement, and computes, that by working six days in the week, instead of four, or twelve hours in the day, instead of eight, he could afford to sell his shoes nearly a third cheaper, he would, by conforming his practice to such a calculation, quickly have the whole trade to himself, and ruin his rivals, if they did not follow his example, and work as diligently as he. This industrious, or avaricious tradesman, having once forced his brother-workmen to be as industrious as himself, the consequence would be, that the quantity of shoes produced would be one third more, or the price one third less. The same reasoning is applicable to every other kind of manufacture; and shews what national wealth might be expected from the lower classes of people, were they but roused to a spirit of industry, and encouraged to amass some little property of their own. One great sign of the opulence of England is the frequent accounts we have, in the public papers, of eminent tallow-chandlers and eminent grocers dying worth twenty thousand and thirty thousand pounds; which opulence is not so much to be computed from the wealth possessed by those individuals, as from the rivalship that must have been produced among their fellow-workmen by their persevering industry.

Most of our writers on commerce take notice of the poverty of Spain, which they attribute to the balance of trade with the other

other European states being continually
against that nation; for they tell us, that
the whole of the gold and silver which the
Spaniards annually draw from their American
colonies does not remain in Spain, but passes
immediately to the commercial nations with
whom the Spaniards trade. Now the very
reason those writers assign for the poverty of
Spain seems to prove it flowing from another
cause; for if Spain can pay her debts to her
European neighbours by the gold and silver
that is annually brought from her American
colonies, she ought herself, at the end of the
year, to be neither poorer nor richer than she
was before. The poverty of Spain then not
being owing to her paying annually a large
commercial balance to foreigners, there must
be some other cause; and I doubt not but
that cause will be found to be the laziness
and idleness of the low people, from which
probably that state suffers an annual loss of
ten millions sterling, that is, she has yearly
ten millions less to spend or to hoard; and
supposing only an annual deficiency of one
million in accumulation, this, in the course
of two centuries, would make her sink in
comparative wealth two hundred millions:
and I question whether this last sum now laid
out in improving her lands, roads, harbours,
villages, towns, manufactures, &c. would
bring her up to an equality with England at
present. But besides this loss in accumulation, arising from the idleness of the working
hands, there is another annual loss, from
the same cause, of nine millions, in the daily
expence for what may be called transitory
wants, which must render the number of
wretched and miserable very great in Spain,

that

that is, the number of those who have nothing, or not a sufficiency to spend; and the
revenues of the state, which ought to have
increased from the accumulation as well as
by the transitory expence, must suffer a deficiency of at least two millions annually from
that neglect of industry among the lower classes
of the people.

Happily for Ireland, there is another spirit
in the government of that island than in the
government of Spain. The warmest patriotic
zeal has long animated the legislature of Ireland ; and maxims having a tendency to
promote the prosperity of the island are
adopted and pursued by them with activity
and perseverance. I cannot help remarking,
however, that several prejudices still subsist
among many people there, which hinder
them from perceiving the true causes of
the unimproved state of the island, or make
them believe that insurmountable obstacles
lie in the way of its prosperity. Among
those prejudices, the chief may be reckoned
that relating to the absentees, and another,
which attributes the poverty of Ireland to
the scarcity of cash, or small quantity of circulating money. The first of these has already been set in a new, and, I hope, in a true
light, so as to prove the drain from absentees
not peculiar to Ireland ; but a drain common
to every distant member of a great empire,
interwoven with the very essence of all monarchical states, and, when not excessive, no
ways detrimental to their highest prosperity.
The other, regarding the small quantity of
cash in circulation, is more the complaint of
the slothful than of the industrious ; and if the
former of these be numerous in a nation, the

complaint

complaint will be very general, but may not for all that be juft. Individuals are counted rich according to the quantity of money they poffefs or can command; but it is not always fo with ftates, or I may venture to fay, it is never fo: for were the Englifh or the Dutch to be as idle as fome nations are, diftrefs and mifery would prevail among them, in fpite of their accumulated heaps of gold, nay, would even be more feverely felt on account of thofe heaps. The flothful has as many wants to fupply as the induftrious; but difliking to have recourfe to the fund of affiduous labour, which is a rich mine to the other, he lays the blame of his diftreffes upon the general want of money in the country, never reflecting, that if the quantity of money fhould be doubled, or even quadrupled, if he did not alter his manner of life, and apply to induftry, a very fmall proportion of the augmented wealth would fall to his fhare, and he would feel his wants ftill more preffing than before. The idea that national poverty was connected with the fcarcity of gold and filver, and that national wealth would be the confequence of poffeffing thofe metals, has long ago been prevalent in Ireland, as appears from the following paffage of a very judicious author on trade, who wrote in the beginning of this century. " We need go " no further, he fays, than our neighbouring " kingdom* of Ireland to fhew the delufion " of being rich with other people's money. " After the laft war, in 1697, when the coin " was raifed to a ftandard in England, it was " raifed, very imprudently, about twenty per " cent- above it in Ireland, upon which, Ire- " land filled with money, more than they
" had

" had ufe for; but as foon as guineas fell
" from twenty-fix to twenty-three, and the
" other coins in proportion, they who tum-
" bled in their money carried it out as faft,
" and left Ireland as it is, thus poor to a pro-
" verb: and fo it will fare with any country
" that fancies itfelf rich with borrowed mo-
" ney." (See Sir Francis Brewfter's Effays
on Trade, 1702). This author fpeaks of a
period but five years later than the fettlement
of Ireland by king William, after a ruinous
civil war, when agriculture, commerce, and
manufactures were at a very low ftate in that
ifland, and when the refource of paper currency was not fo much as known there. All
thefe circumftances muft doubtlefs have occafioned a great deal of diftrefs among the
people of Ireland, but they certainly grafped
at a fhadow, when they thought of removing that diftrefs by rating gold and filver
twenty per cent more than their neighbours;
nay, perhaps, forty per cent more, by not
only taking the metals at a higher valuation;
but, probably, paying for them an intereft one
fifth higher than that paid by their neighbours.

The notion that money of gold and filver
is abfolutely effential for the profperity of a
ftate, may in fact become the means of keep-
ing a ftate poor, by preventing the inhabitants from adverting to the real fources of
their riches, and inducing them to give a
high price, or pay very dear for an inftru-
ment of commerce, which they can actually
do without. In the reign of queen Elizabeth
gold and filver could not be borrowed, but
at an intereft of ten per cent†. which was a

D 2 .   tax

---

† From whence arofe the proverb in lord Bacon's time, *That the
devil had his tythes as well as the clergy.* It is not much more than feventy years fince money was at ten per cent. in Ireland.

tax of a third or a fourth upon the profit of
the borrower, fuppofing him to make thirty,
or forty per cent advantage in confequence
of his loan. Should only two millions have
been lent at that intereft in queen Elizabeth's
time, it would have created a yearly burden
upon induftry of two hundred thoufand
pounds heavier than the fupplies then raifed
annually for the government; two thirds of
which burden the induftrious might have
got rid of by having recourfe to another me-
dium of commerce. This expedient would
have been thought impoffible in thofe days;
but fact and experience, in modern times,
juftify the practicability and great utility of
it. Suppofing a number of monied men
were to carry their cafh to fome of our colonies in America, and gracioufly offer the
inhabitants the ufe of their money at an intereft of ten per cent, as the means of quickly enriching the colony, the colonifts might
juftly reply to thofe monied men, " We re-
" gard a fertile foil as the one thing need-
" ful for the fuftenance of life. Let us but
" have that, and with it and our own in-
" duftry, we do not defpair of enriching
" ourfelves and our pofterity without the
" immediate affiftance of gold and filver;
" therefore, as we find we can do without
" your money, you may carry it to thofe
" who fet a value upon it, or fee if you can
" extract from it food and cloathing as we
" can from our lands." Moft of our American colonifts, if we regard their manner of
conducting their internal commerce, give in
fact this reply by their actions. They have,
within thefe hundred years, extracted above
two hundred millions from their lands, built
many

many cities, launched thoufands of fhips, acquired large ftocks of cattle, and much other
fubftance, with very little aid from gold and
filver; and were all other communities ac-
tuated by the fame fpirit, the monied men
would find themfelves exactly in the fituation of Midas, and fee the induftrious well
cloathed and well fed, while they themfelves
were ftarving.

Few countries on the globe in the northern
latitudes afford fuch refources of wealth from
the fertility of the foil as Ireland affords; yet
by far too great a proportion of the lands
of that ifland are lying much in the fame
ftate as they were left by the flood of Noah.
The people, inftead of beftowing attention
upon that immenfe annual lofs keep up the
cry of ruin on account of the fcarcity of cafh,
and fome years ago were filled with the greateft alarms, and looked upon themfelves as
on the point of perdition, from a threatened
importation of brafs halfpence, a puny evil,
which muft in its very operation foon have
corrected itfelf, though not one fyllable had
ever been written againft it. Ireland, though
inhabited from the greateft antiquity, is quite
a young commercial ftate; therefore, as no
gold and filver mines are wrought in that
country, it is not in the leaft furprifing to
find a fcarcity of thofe metals there, which
only abound in ftates that have had for a
long courfe of years a lucrative commerce,
without the exhaufting drain of expenfive
foreign wars. The commercial exiftence of Ireland can hardly be traced farther back than
that of our American colonies, and even now
its trade cannot, properly fpeaking, be faid to
have acquired fuch a maturity as that of the
colonifts,

colonifts, when we confider the fhameful deficiency of fhipping in that ifland, the reproach of which is, in part, owing to impolitic regulations, and imprudent counfels in
Great Britain. The Irifh have, no doubt,
bought and fold with their neighbours for
ages paft, but not with the fyftematic view
of accumulation and profit, that has pre-
vailed fince the Revolution, to the great advantage of the ifland, . which has more than
doubled its ftock of wealth fince that period,
without adding in the leaft, perhaps, to its
quantity of gold and filver. The flothful
and difcontented keep their eyes upon this
laft circumftance, and will not fee the former,
which is by far the moft effential.

Were they, however, but properly to confider the confequences arifing from a fmall
ftock of money in circulation, inftead of
looking on it as a caufe of difcouragement,.
they would draw from it one of the greateft
incitements to induftry. Every thing to be
purchafed at home. if they are but induftrious, will be purchafed the cheaper for it.
Were the expence of living equal in both
iflands, many more land proprietors would
be tempted to crowd to London; but while
Dublin continues lefs luxurious, and lefs expenfive than the capital of Great Britain,
Irifh families, of good fortunes, if they have
children to provide for, will chufe not to
quit Ireland, which will prevent the drain of
abfentees from becoming exceffive†. High

† Some people at Dublin, to prove the opulence and the flourifh-
ing ftate of Ireland, have vaunted that living was as dear at that
capital as at London, which, if true, would be a real caufe of la-
mentation to the Irifn, and not of boafting; for nothing could happen more prejudicial to Ireland than fuch an equality, which ought
to be prevented by every kind of attention on the part of the Irifh.
With the fame judgment, fome people give it as a proof of England's
being the richeft country in Europe, becaufe it is the deareft.

wages, and high perfection in the arts, are no more necessarily connected together, than national poverty is with a small quantity of gold and silver. Do the people of Geneva sell the fewer watches, because they sell them cheap, that is, because they work for low wages? On the contrary, the very circumstance of cheapness, occasions so great a demand for watches from thence, that a full third of the inhabitants of the republic, or about thirteen thousand people, (two or three thousand of whom are women,) gain their livelihood by that branch of manufacture. Were the great masters in painting, who flourished in Italy two or three hundred years ago, inferior in merit to our modern portrait painters, because they did not receive so much for five or six of their performances as ours gain by one of theirs? Are the porcelaine manufactures in China, or the weavers in the East Indies less skilful than ours, because they work for two-pence and three-pence a day? These few instances, not to mention many others, may serve to shew the falseness of that maxim, that cheap countries are consequently and necessarily poor countries, where the arts must absolutely languish. A cheap country is, to an enterprising manufacturer, the same thing as new soil to a skilful planter or farmer. Both give the most just expectation of the richest returns of industry. What, but the cheapness of countries, first drew the hardware manufacture to Birmingham, and the great woollen manufacture to Yorkshire and Westmoreland? What fixes the glass works at Newcastle and Bristol, but the cheapness of firing, an article that makes great part of the expence of glass.

Now

Now among an induſtrious people, what elſe is cheapneſs or lowneſs of wages, than, *the having a great deal of labour for a ſmall quantity of money?* And can any circumſtance be more favourable than this to a nation, that has manufactures to carry to a foreign market, where they may meet with a competition with the manufactures of other nations? Where two ſtates offer merchandize of equal goodneſs, that ſtate which can ſell the cheapeſt, will not only be ſure of the readieſt market, but will in all probability gain more by what it ſells, than the other ſtate which ſells dear. Great Britain being obliged, on account of her immenſe national debt, to keep up an exceſſive circulation, has thereby rendered proviſions and wages ſo dear, that ſhe has in a great degree precluded herſelf from foreign markets; and this dearneſs is far from being owing to the over great plenty of ſilver and gold; for were all her paper money but ſuppreſſed for three or four months, the moſt preſuming of the opulence of Great Britain would ſoon be convinced of the abſolute ſcarcity of real caſh. The immenſity of her taxes, however, renders this artificial aid in circulation at preſent neceſſary, and her merchants muſt fight their way in foreign markets in the beſt manner they can, though it be probable their commiſſions from abroad would be doubled, could they afford their merchandize at lower prices. Whatever eagerneſs foreigners expreſs for Britiſh manufactures, the dearneſs of thoſe manufactures damps their ardour for purchaſing them. I remember a very enterpriſing foreign retailer, who had received a quantity of Birmingham goods, which he much admired, being greatly

ly

ly panded, nevertheless, with the invoice, the articles of which were written in French, and the sums specified in English money. He was hugging himself with the thoughts of a great bargain, and was forming plans of large dealings with England, having interpreted the £. and the *s.* in the invoice into livres and sols; but when those letters were explained to him as denoting pounds and shillings, (three and twenty times more than he had imagined) the utmost amazement was visible on his countenance, and he immediately said that he must write directly to his correspondent, to send him no more goods, as he feared he should not be able to sell those he had already received. Thus Great Britain, by her superabonce of wealth, has in a great degree cut herself off from dealing to advantage with her poorer neighbours; but this is not a situation to be envied by Ireland. On the contrary, nothing could be more unfortunate for the Irish, than to have money as abundant in their island as it is in England; and indeed while England makes a branch of a sovereignty, it is not in the nature of things that money should be so plentiful there as in the provinces near the center of government, which is at the same time the center of commerce. But it does not follow from thence that poverty and misery should prevail in Ireland, as an acre may be equally prolific and fertile when rented at a shilling as when let at a guinea, and a manufacturer, who labours diligently twelve hours a day, will finish the same quantity of work, whether his wages be six pence a day or half a crown. The capital maxim to be observed in Ireland is, that the rents of the lands should

E   bear

bear a proportion to the small quantity of currency; and in this view there seems to have been no less of sound policy than of humanity in the order sent home by lord Charlemont, when he was absent on his travels, NOT to raise the rents of his tenants. If lands and industry in Ireland are too much neglected, money is there too much esteemed, I mean trade is there burdened by the too high rate of the interest of money, when, as I have above observed, the present period affords a most constitutional expedient for reducing that rate to four or even three per cent. There is neither so much trade, nor so much money in the duchy of Tuscany as in Ireland, yet at this very time the three per cents, at Florence are sold above par. Were the interest of money reduced in Ireland, and the poor people to enjoy a settled comfortable life, free from vexations and from burdensome takes, abundance would soon be more generally diffused, from their application to industry, and their confidence in the secure possession of their own labour. In this case the complaints of the want of cash might soon be turned into boastings of the cheapness of living, which contributes as much to the advancement of population, and the attracting of strangers, as the opinion of high wages; witness the frequent emigrants to America, who generally assign that as the cause of their voluntary transportation. But the wants of mankind are of more kinds than one. Real abundance consists in having manufactures at easy prices, as well as food; and the legislature of Ireland, with proper attention, and by making an alteration in the modes of taxation, might promote this two fold plenty much

much more generally throughout the island, without any augmentation of the present currency.

The throwing too much of the public burdens upon the poor, and exempting lands from taxes, is greatly detrimental to the state in another view than that of checking the industry of manufacturers and labourers. The indolent land-proprietor of two or three hundred a year, who lives upon his estate, who kills his own meat, brews his own beer, bakes his own bread, makes his own candles, &c. is a subject, who, by the present mode of taxation, lives very uselessly for the state, as the government can draw very little, either from him or his property, three fourths of which perhaps lies unimproved, or in a state of nature, which is an essential loss to the public. Take a number of journeymen in a manufacturing town, whose revenues together are but equal to that of the above-mentioned landholder, and it will be found that their share of the public taxes is twice as great as his, the state at the same time being enriched by their industry to four or five times the amount of the taxes paid by them. Such a landholder, by his manner of life, not only contributes little to the public burdens, but actually keeps the nation from thriving; for, by suffering his wide domain to lie in a state of nature, when, by proper cultivation in the hands of wealthy tenants, it might be made to yield four or five times as much, he obstructs the improvement of territory, which is the greatest of all national improvements. Would it not rather be an advantage than a detriment to the state to tax the lands of such a proprietor, and would not trade be

greatly

greatly advanced, if landlords of finall
properties, who now live idly upon their
estates, were induced to betake themselves
to commerce or manufactures, in the easy
profecution of which, their land-revenues
would not a' little affift them? This we fee
often practifed in England and in France;
and manufacturers or merchants, who traffic
with fuch stocks, can certainly afford to fell
cheaper, and pufh a more extenfive trade,
than thofe who carry on commerce with borrowed funds. Whatever tends to diminifh
the number of *workers*, and the increafe the number of *wafters*, hurts a state; but few things
have a greater tendency to promote both
thefe, than to encourage, by an almoft total
exemption from public burdens, landlords of
finall properties to live idly, and to breed up
their families in the fame manner of living.

From what has been written above, I think
it plainly appears, that the people of Ireland
are far from being fo poor as they imagine
themfelves to be, from their finall stock of
currency; and likewife, that they are not fo
burdened, either by their taxes or their abfentees, as they generally believe. That the wealth
of Ireland does not correfpond with the extent and fertility of her territory, with the
riches of her furrounding feas, and her conve-
nient fituation for foreign commerce, every
one acquainted with that ifland will moft
readily allow; but I am far from attributing
that to heavy taxation, to the drains of abfentees, or to the finall quantity of cafh. It
is much more applicable to the claffing and
animofity of different religions, which have
dulled the hand of hufbandry, to the very
uncultivated state of the lands, to the high
                                        interest

interest of money, to discouraging leases,
to the want of dock-yards and ship carpenters, and the employment of foreign ships,
to the luxurious indulgence in foreign products and manufactures, to injudicious taxes,
and above all to a partially limited foreign
trade.

This last is certainly the greatest grievance
of all others, and has long been a reproach
to the counsels of Great Britain; for while
it has subsisted, it may very justly be said,
to have been attended with no less prejudice
to this island than to Ireland. That ill founded narrow principle of conforming our commercial regulations to the Dutch model,
misled some of our politicians in the last century, to make the absurd supposition, that
our circumstances might be bettered, if half
our territory were destroyed, that is, if what
yielded us annually the value of fifteen millions were annihilated. It was better, according to them, to fetch corn from Poland,
than to have it of our own growth, better to bring black cattle by sea from the Bal-
tic, or the coast of the Adriatic, than to
drive them from our own mountains. The
Dutch, they said, were acquiring opulence
and power, and were amassing wealth faster,
and in a higher degree, than any other state
in Europe : therefore happy the state that
could imitate them, and put itself in their
situation, which would raise it to a degree of
eminence superior to what it could expect
from a large and fertile territory; though
they alledged nothing to prove that maxims of industry might not prevail in the large
territory, as well as in the narrow swamp;
and totally overlooked the wealth that nature

spontaneously

spontaneoufly produces from territory alone,
independent of the induftry of man, which is
fometimes one third of the wealth of a ftate.
The Dutch, at this moment, are finking in their
importance in Europe, from the very caufe
formerly affigned by our political writers for
their opulence and grandeur, I mean the narrownefs of territory; and their immenfe
ftocks of money, their number of fhips, and
their populous towns will not be able to fecure them againft a ftill farther decline,
fhould their maritime neighbours become
more active in commerce, and appropriate to
themfelves their natural advantages. Should
Great Britain affert the fame exclufive right
of fifhing in her feas at home, as fhe has fe-
cured in the feas of Newfoundland; and
fhould other European nations imitate her
example in that particular; fhould all the
different fpices of the Eaft be raifed in the
Britifh, French, and Spanifh Weft Indies;
and fhould each nation be the carrier of its
own merchandize, the power and opulence
of the Dutch would foon become proportioned to the narrownefs and badnefs of their
territory, notwithftanding the utmoft efforts
of induftry on the part of the inhabitants.
The hiftories of paft ages moft plainly de-
clare, that power, founded on commerce in
a narrow territory, has always been preca-
rious and tranfitory; neverthelefs the fplen-
did period of the Dutch republic fo dazzled
the minds of many people in England, that
they forgot their own natural advantages to
over-rate theirs, and could they but acquire
commerce, were not follicitous within what
narrow limits it was reftrained, falfely efteem-
ing the balance of wealth procured by trade

before the advantages arising from widening
the circle of induſtry over a fertile ſoil, pof-
ſeſſing above three thouſand miles of ſea-
coaſt.

What ſhould we think of the governments
of France and Spain, ſhould they lay penal
reſtrictions upon one third of their provinces,
in regard to induſtry and trade, with a view
of procuring an accumulation of wealth to
the other two thirds. The commoneſt ob-
ſerver, upon reading ſuch an article of intelligence in a gazette, ſuppoſing him a Britiſh
ſubject, might make the following comment
upon it. This is a circumſtance extremely
favourable to Great Britain. The French and
Spaniards, by ſuch a political regulation, will
moſt effectually check their own powers for
the provinces thus laid under penal reſtrictions, whatever natural advantages they pof-
ſeſs, muſt neceſſarily languiſh, and yield much
leſs profit to the whole than they would
otherwiſe do; and in the favoured provinces,
things will ſoon riſe to ſuch high prices, and
manufactures will become ſo dear, that they
will no longer rival ours in foreign markets,
or be poured in upon us by our ſmugglers.
While the French and Spaniards continue
thus blind to their own intereſt, they will
become every day leſs objects of jealouſy
to us.

But it is not the French and the Spaniards
who act thus imprudently; it is the inhabitants of Great Britain. What muſt the
French and Spaniards think of us, when they
ſee us neglect one third of our provinces,
while our foreign trade is actually threatened
with a ſtagnation in the other two thirds, on
account of the exceſſive dearneſs of proviſions

fions and labour? Though Ireland, on account of its vicinity to us, and its fubjection to the fame fovereign authority with ourfelves, ought to have been confidered merely as a part of Great Britain, and a very confiderable part, our legiflature has neverthelefs moft impolitically neglected the interefts of Ireland, from a falfe perfuafion of thereby advancing the interefts of this ifland. But the advancing the intereft of both iflands, as one object, ought ever to have been the point aimed at in all general deliberations of Great Britain. A commercial nation, that would wifh to fecure a permanent grandeur, muft found her power on the board bafis of territory, every part of which territory ought proportionally to enjoy the advantages arifing from the commercial balance. When the nourifhment, that is, when induftry and commerce, are juftly diftributed, all the parts become vigorous, and the ftrength of the whole will daily encreafe, till it bear a proportion to the extent of the territory, nay, may even exceed that proportion, and ftill be counted natural, if the territory be bounded every where by the fea, and have on all fides numbers of excellent ports.

Thefe laft circumftances are wholly applicable to the natural fituation of Great Britain and Ireland; and were our commerce to be regulated by them, it might be rendered much more extenfive and more lucrative, and confequently the collective ftrength of both iflands be greatly augmented. But now the political as well as the natural fituation of Great Britain and Ireland points out to us the urgent neceffity of a communication of commercial advantages to the latter ifland; and

fhews

shews most plainly, that to persevere in the present system of exclusion would be the height of impolicy. Great Britain ought no longer to regard Ireland as a rival Sister, but as a joint Parent of America; in which case Ireland would soon have a parent's concern, and would concur with pleasure in maintaining our and her own rights and interests in that part of the world against every European disturber. The time, I say, is at length arrived for a total change of system in regard to Ireland; and, therefore, the legislature of Great Britain will now, most undoubtedly, advance the prosperity of both islands, by enacting, in conjunction with the legislature of the neighbouring kingdom, That the foreign trade of Ireland be, in every respect, put upon the same footing as the foreign trade of Great Britain; That the duties laid in either kingdom, upon the products or manufactures of the other, be reciprocally suppressed and abolished; and that all vessels sailing from one island to the other be considered as coasting vessels, and be subject only to the same regulations as such vessels are subject to; that the communication and trade between Ireland and the British settlements in America and Africa, be put upon the same footing as the trade between Great Britain and those settlements; That, in consideration of this general liberty of trade, the kingdom of Ireland shall always pay for the support of government, and the public defence of the state, a land-tax of equal rate with the land tax of Great Britain for the time being; That the denominations and the value of the denominations of money shall be the same in both kingdoms; That the port duties or customs upon all merchandize, exported or imported, be

F

the

the fame in Ireland as in Great Britain; That the rate of the interest of money be reduced in Ireland; That the additional taxes, raised as an equivalent for a freedom of trade, be always appropriated to the building of ships of war, and the maintaining and supporting a naval strength in Ireland, &c. These, and such other regulations as may appear most fitting to the prudence of each legislature for putting both islands upon a perfect equality in respect to foreign trade, would soon animate industry in Ireland, and consequently increase her annual income, and render her of much more advantage to Great Britain than she is at present.

I am very sensible, that the proposal I have made of granting a freedom of trade to Ireland, will have many prejudices and partial interests to encounter with; but I am at the same time persuaded, that those who will impartially weigh the present state of both islands, will most readily acknowledge both the *equity* and the *expediency* of such a freedom of trade. Old prejudices ought to have no weight, when the causes that gave rise to them have ceased: and all partial and private interests ought to yield to the interest of the public, I mean that of the whole community. It would be injurious, some will say, to the inhabitants of this island to put the Irish upon the same footing with them in regard to foreign trade, since the Irish do not bear such heavy public burdens as the former, that is, do not contribute so amply to the general charges of the state. This has been, and is still, the chief and most plausible objection against extending the freedom of trade to Ireland; but as the reasoning contained in it proves too much, it proves nothing; for by

the

the same argument more than the half of
England, with all Scotland, ought to be cut
off from the freedom of trade, since they together do not contribute so much to the
public burdens as the county of Middlesex
joined to fourteen or fifteen other home
counties †. Great Britain, taken collectively,
contributes in a greater proportion to the
public burdens than Ireland, taken in the same
view; but that is owing to the immense circulation and expence of London, the common
capital of the whole empire : and to supporting the excessive expence of that center of
union, Ireland, as a member, contributes her
share, together with the remote parts of England, with Scotland, America, and the East and
West Indies. Ireland, in all our political deliberations, ought to be confidered merely as
a remote part of Great Britain; and if we
examine her public burdens in that view, and
compare them with those levied in any part of
this island at a great distance from the capital,
and of equal extent with Ireland, the dispro-
portion between the Irish and those British
taxes will not be very confiderable. To leffen
that difproportion, and to bring the burdens
in both nearer to an equality, I have propofed
fome augmentation in Ireland, by a land-tax,
to rife and fall as that tax shall rife and fall
in Britain; the moſt equitable, in point of
impofition, and the moſt conducive to for-
ward and promote industry in Ireland. Be-
fides, confidering Ireland merely as a remote

F 2 part

† Such an excluſion would be making one monopoly the caule of
another; for the great proportion of taxes paid by the capital is owing to one fixth of our foreign trade, namely, the East India trade,
being monopolifed by the port of London.

part of Great Britain, it ought, on that very
account, to be more favoured in point of taxation than the provinces near the center of
government, as circulation, both in the natural and political body, is always more lan-
guid towards the extremities than towards
the heart; and wages and rents ought naturally to be always lower in Ireland than in
the countries near London. Should the Irish
then consent to but a small augmentation
of taxes, in that case, they could no longer
be said to stand precluded from the *right to
the freedom of trade.*

The mercantile short sighted policy of con-
fining the woollen manufactures to England,
has likewise been another objection to the extending the freedom of trade to Ireland; and
has, in its consequences, been attended with
many losses and disadvantages to Great Britain, by throwing that branch of manufacture into the hands of our continental rivals,
who hold an interest contrary to ours. Had we
considered Ireland, as in true policy it ought
always to have been considered, merely as
a part of Great Britain, we should never
have thought that the woollen manufacture
moved from home, when we saw a branch
of it flourish in Ireland. Indeed, there ought
to be no more cause of alarm in seeing the
woollen manufacture, or any other manufacture, flourish in Ireland, than in seeing another
Birmingham rise in Suffex, or another Leeds
rise in Dorfetshire. Whoever should urge the
arguments used in King William's time, or
in the time of King Charles II. for justifying
the jealousy of trade in regard to Ireland,
would reason extremely false upon the subject. Those arguments, even then, were far
from

from being conclusive; and had they even
been juft at that period, the political ftate of
both iflands is of late years fo greatly altered,
that they would be fafe now. England, at
that time, might be faid to have hardly any
intercourfe or trade with America, fo incon-
fiderable were the American colonies then,
to what they are at prefent; neither was Scotland then united with her, nor had fhe the
manufactures of filk, of cotton, of hardware,
of linen, of paper, with twenty other kinds,
that have fince taken root and now flourifh
among us. She was then almoft confined to
one fingle fpecies of manufacture: namely,
the woollen, the market for which, both foreign and domeftic, was twice as extenfive as
at prefent. In thofe times, our ladies wore
ftuffs; now, even our very fervant maids are
cloathed in filks and cottons. The fame alteration has taken place in moft of the nations
abroad; and even in the filk countries, the
confumption of filks is much more confiderable
at prefent than it was an hundred years ago;
all of which circumftances have contributed to
make the woollen manufacture an object of
much lefs importance in thefe days than it
was in former times. The Englifh, in the
laft century, having in a manner but one manufacture, and being totally unacquainted
with any other, faw nothing but mifery and
poverty, fhould they be rivalled in that by
their neighbours of Ireland, whom they very
falfely confidered as people with hoftile in-
tentions, wifhing for nothing fo much as to
have a religion and intereft to themfelves.
The bitter animofity manifefted in the late
religious civil wars gave fome colour to fuch
a fufpicion, efpecially as England could not
then

then depend upon the joint affiftance of Scotland, and had then no Eaft and Weft India revenue; and Ireland, joined to the great advantage of low wages, a fuperfluous abundance of the firft material. What a dif-, ferent figure does Great Britain now make, with lands Improved from one extremity of the ifland to the other, with amazingly ex-, tenfive and wide-fpreading colonies, that ab- folutely demand an enlargement of the trunk that is to fuftain and fupport them, with not one manufacture alone, but with many, brought to great perfection, and an af- fured market for them among her American fubjects; and how different, likewife, is the ftate of Ireland from what it was in former times!

· The cruel civil war, of nine years conti- nuance, had fo exhaufted Ireland, that in the beginning of the reign of Charles II. it had the air of a new fettled colony. The oppofite parties, not contented with fhedding each other's blood, had fpitefully flaughtered each other's cattle, which foon introduced a fa- mine, that proved more wafteful than the fword. If we add to thofe two calamities the defertion of great numbers of inhabitants, it may juftly be concluded, that at the fettle- ment by Cromwell there was hardly half the number of people in the ifland that there is in it at prefent. It feems to have been fettled then much in the fame manner as we now fettle the colony of Florida. The grants of the adventurers, for want of inhabitants, were difpofed of at the greateft undervalua- tion; and, to procure tenants and cultivators, many leafes of lands were granted for terms of ninety-nine years, at a groat an acre; fome

of

of which leafes have, of late years, been re-
newed, at a guinea an acre. Other inftances
might be produced to prove the great depo-
pulation of the iſland at what is called its fer-
tlement after the civil war. When tranquil-
lity was reſtored, improvement would immediately take place; but ſtocks of people are not
ſo eaſily nor ſo quickly recruited as ſtocks of
cattle and ſheep, which laſt, we find, were then
exported thither, in great numbers, from England: the conſequence of which was, that Ireland was ſoon over-run with herds and flocks,
and had much more wool and proviſions
than her ſmall number of inhabitants could
conſume. Wages being then extremely low,
in conſequence of the great lowneſs of rents,
it was moſt natural for the Iriſh to think of
turning their ſuperfluity to advantage, and
for the Engliſh, from the falſe maxims of
policy that then filled their minds, to look
upon them as formidable rivals, never ſuſ-
pecting that rivals truly formidable might
ſtart up in other quarters. Ireland, in its
modern ſtate, preſents us with a very different proſpect. The number of its inhabitants is doubled, conſequently the home-
conſumption of its wool and proviſions muſt
likewiſe be doubled; and therefore the diſ-
proportion between the people and the flocks
cannot now be ſo great as formerly, ſince
much more land muſt now be occupied by
tillage, both for corn and flax, and the great
luxury in horſes, ſo much increaſed of late
years, demands a conſiderable part of the
paſturage to be appropriated for them. The
Iriſh are endeavouring yearly to throw more
of their lands into tillage, as they now
ſee the great impolicy of growing a
ſufficient

sufficient quantity of corn for their own subsistence; and should they succeed in that œconomical plan, and should a free and enlarged trade increase the number of their people, and raise the value of their lands, we should soon hear no more of the superabundance or cheapness, either of their cattle or their wool, as they would, on this last supposition, still require a greater quantity of both for their own consumption, and the value of land being raised, would raise the prices of what the farmer brought to the market.

The breeders of cattle in the grazing counties in Great Britain will likewise cry out, that their interests will be affected upon allowing a freedom of importation from Ireland; but if we appeal to experience, we may safely affirm, that they need not be greatly alarmed on this subject; for I may ask, if the gentlemen of the grazing counties in England found themselves sensibly injured immediately after the union with Scotland, when the southern market was opened for Scotch cattle, which have ever since been sent into England in numbers ten times greater than can ever be expected to come from Ireland, should a free communication be opened between Great Britain and that island? When all obstructions to the mutual commerce of the two islands are removed, the prices of things, of course, will gradually approach near to an equality in both countries, which will greatly promote the ease of living through the whole; for it is not for the interest of a state that any one county, or any one part, should possess an artificial advantage over the others. It is the improving the

the natural advantages that best promotes the general welfare. The breeding of horses is much more lucrative than the breeding of cattle; but the excessive dearness of butcher-meat seems to prove that the soil of Great Britain does not suffice for breeding both in the degree that our wants require for home-consumption and exportation. If we would wish, therefore, to continue the advantageous commerce of the exportation of horses, and at the same time have provisions at moderate prices, we ought, without delay, to allow the free importation of Irish cattle, by which expedient, the labouring poor would be enabled to live upon their present wages, while the profits of the landed gentlemen in general would not be in the least abased. Whoever considers the traffic for cattle and sheep carried on between Scotland and England, must acknowledge, that it is extremely advantageous both to the northern and southern parts of this island; but no reason can be given in favour of that traffic, that does not equally plead for opening a communication of the same kind between Ireland and Great Britain. That the want of such a communication was a great prejudice to England, was the opinion of one of the ablest of our political writers†, who makes it a query, " Whether it would " not be best for both kingdoms to take off " the prohibition that now lies on Irish cattle ? " —It remains very doubtful, he says, when " this prohibition was set on foot, which was " most consulted, public good or private " interest, the numbers of the breeding " were, without doubt, stronger at that time " than those of the feeding lands. But it is " to be feared, in the making that act, that

G   " the

---

† See Davenant's Political Works, vol. II. p. 152. Whitworth's edition.

" the general intereſt of England was not
" ſufficiently conſidered." If the free ad-
miſſion of Iriſh cattle would have promoted
the intereſt of England ſeventeen years ago,
as may be plainly inferred from the words of
Davenant, there ſeems much ſtronger reaſon
to conclude, that ſuch an importation, in the
preſent period, would be extremely beneficial
to this iſland, and would effect more in bring-
ing proviſions to moderate prices, and keep-
ing them ſo, than can be expected from the
moſt patriotic ſubſcription for that purpoſe,
the conſequences of which, it is to be feared,
will be only temporary.

But all the objections to the propoſed regulations for a freedom of trade to Ireland
will not be on the ſide of the inhabitants of
Great Britain : the intereſted in Ireland will
likewiſe have their objections to ſome clauſes,
particularly to that for ſuppreſſing and abo-
liſhing the duties laid in either kingdom upon
the products and manufactures of the other.
This article, they will alledge, will open a
door to the exceſſive importation of Engliſh
manufactures into Ireland, to the detriment
of the manufactures of that country. The
clauſe is certainly meant to promote the in-
tercourſe between the inhabitants of both
iſlands ; for when I mentioned the exceſſive
indulgence in foreign products and manufactures, as one of the reaſons of the low ſtate
of Ireland, I was far from intending to
rank the products and manufactures of Great
Britain as foreign in Ireland : on the contrary, I am moſt fully perſuaded, that it
would be for the advantage of both iſlands
that

that nothing belonging to the one should be looked upon as foreign in the other. Allowing that the clause will contribute to increase the sale of English manufactures in Ireland, it will nevertheless have many other consequences, besides that, which ought also to be taken into the account, and which, on the whole, will most undoubtedly tend to the advantage of Ireland separately, as well as collectively with Great Britain. By this clause, Irish manufactures, that are now prohibited in Great Britain, would be importable hither; and Irish products, also prohibited, would have a new, and, at the same time, a most free and extensive market, with hardly any risk of sea. And by a subsequent clause in the same proposed regulation, tobacco, sugar, rum, and other products of the American colonies, may be brought directly into Ireland; by which the Irish will be gainers in a double respect, first, in having those articles cheaper, and next, in raising the same public revenue from the importation of them as is raised in Great Britain. But in such an intricate subject as this, we can best of all judge of what may happen by what has happened. When we have the experience of a similar case before our eyes, the consequences we would draw from the present have then a degree of certainty equal to demonstration. At the union of England and Scotland, did either kingdom suffer when the barriers that obstructed mutual commerce were broke down? Did not both, on the contrary, gain by the open communication? Before that period, the prohibitions were extremely rigorous in both kingdoms, in regard to each others products and manufactures;

but

but though Scotland now confumes ten times more of Englifh manufactures than fhe did feventy years ago, and her abfentees are an hundred times more numerous; fo far from being impoverifhed by thofe two feemingly alarming circumftances, fhe is increafed in riehes, people, and manufactures, confiderably. We may be confident, therefore, that the fame thing would happen to the Irifh, were every prohibition and reftraint removed in the mutual commerce of the two iflands, and a general freedom of trade granted to Ireland.

Many people in Ireland, from interefted or from narrow views, will alfo be ready to object to that article propofing the port-duties, or cuftoms, to be the fame in both kingdoms upon all merchandize exported or imported. Such an article, it may be faid, would alter the prefent channels of commerce to the Irifh, and deprive them of fome markets, where it is generally fuppofed they trade to advantage. But it ought to be remembered, that a freedom of trade cannot be granted to the Irifh without fuch a condition, which, if it would bar up fome channels of trade to them, would open others equally lucrative, and much more natural. Without fuch a condition there could be no equality, and confequently no freedom of trade between Great Britain and Ireland; for many foreign commercial articles, now in a manner prohibited in Great Britain, have a very eafy entry into Ireland; and it would be abfurd to eftablifh a reciprocal freedom of trade between the two iflands, and fuffer foreign articles, the importation of which into Great Britain is deemed prejudicial to our interefts, to be freely imported
into

Into Ireland, from whence they could be so
easily introduced into this island. The Irish,
however, in exchanging some of their present
channels of trade for others, would not only
be gainers in procuring, upon that condition,
a general freedom of trade, but would also
gain considerably in the very change of the
markets. For example, in the great staple
article of provisions, the British market, with
that of the West Indies, would certainly be
ample equivalents for any diminutions in the
markets in France, Spain, and other foreign
countries, where they now trade. Should
French wines, and some other foreign articles
of luxury become somewhat dearer in Ireland
upon such a revolution, many other articles
would become cheaper; and the latter may
be set to counterbalance the former. The
sunshine of arts and industry is in a manner
spread over only one half of Ireland; and
two of her provinces may, at this very day,
be called provinces of France, as much as
provinces of Great Britain. This unnatural
connexion with France, so detrimental both
to Ireland and Great Britain, has certainly
been promoted by the imprudent restraints
laid here upon the trade of Ireland; and
what do the Irish chiefly gain by this connec-
tion? That their low people may riot in poor
French claret, the consumption of which is
too much encouraged over the whole island,
on account of its cheapness, which has served
as a premium to bring it within the reach of
those who, from their stations in life, would
otherwise in all probability, have been contented with home-brewed liquors. Were
the Irish, instead of trading so largely with
France, to have a free trade to Great Britain

a [ ]

and to the British West Indies, with back-freights of sugar and rum from thence, directly to Ireland, the consumption of rum would greatly increase in that island, and might in time superfede the consumption of French wines, to the great advantage of our West India islands. It is universally allowed, that an extension of our sugar colonies would tend to enlarge the trade of Great Britain with foreign nations ; and yet, by impolitic restraints thrown upon Ireland, we in a manner deprive our sugar-colonies of that market, and force the Irish to a very general consumption of foreign sugars. If the North Americans are suffered to carry home sugars, rum, and molasses, without restraint, and no inconveniences have been alledged to attend that commerce, it is certainly full time for us to awaken from our lethargic dream, and to permit a free intercourse between Ireland and all our American settlements; and in that case it might be expected, that the Irish merchants, though they might at first have some repugnance in quitting their old and accustomed channels of commerce, would soon find the new trade proposed more fitted to the prosperity of Ireland, more lucrative to themselves, and much more conducive to advance the strength and grandeur of the British empire in general.

The lowering the rate of the interest of money in Ireland, is no less necessary for the prosperity of that island than a general freedom of trade; and is proposed as an article in the above commercial regulations, with the double view of promoting industry in Ireland, and of obtaining a further reduction of interest in Great Britain, which operation

ration will be greatly facilitated by a previous reduction of interest in Ireland. About twelve years hence an opportunity will offer for reducing a confiderable part of the public debts of Great Britain to two, or two and an half per cent; but, if interest is fuffered to continue high in Ireland, it will be very difficult, or next to impoffible for Great Britain to draw all the advantage from that opportunity, which it will otherwife afford. Public credit in Ireland, has not yet put on the fetters of the monied men; therefore the legiflature of that ifland, by a moft conftitutional expedient, may eafily reduce the legal rate of intereft to three, or four per cent. which would be attended with many happy confequences, both to the landed gentleman and merchant, and foon give additional vigour to the ftate. In proportion to the fucceffive reductions of intereft in Great Britain, has induftry thriven in this ifland, and its power and opulence is increafed. The confequences of thofe reductions have been fo evident, both in regard to the public and to the advancement of trade, that it is now in a manner the general fentiment among all ranks of people, that the lownefs of the rate of intereft contributes to advance the profperity of the nation. From fome unhappy circumftances, however, or fome inadvertence in our government, the fpace of time that has elapfed fince the laft reduction of intereft is much greater than that between the two preceding reductions, and we, who were wont to precede fome of our neighbours in that regulation, have lately fuffered them to precede us; for both the French and Auftrians, fince the conclufion of the late peace,

have

have reduced the rate of intereſt in their dominions to four per cent. Thoſe operations, in ſtates where trade and currency are far from being ſo conſiderable as in Great Britain, ought to awaken us to embrace every favourable opportunity of effecting a farther reduction of intereſt in this kingdom. Ireland at preſent affords ſuch an opportunity; and a conſiderable reduction of intereſt in that kingdom, ſo very practicable at this period, would demonſtrate the eaſy practicability of effecting the ſame in Great Britain, when the occaſion ſhould arive. The obſervation of the ingenious Dr. Price, in regard to ſurpluſes from a high intereſt employed in reducing a capital, accumulating, faſter than ſurpluſes from a low intereſt, is nothing but a mere arithmetical computation, and, as ſuch, is extremely juſt; but it is far from following from thence, that it is for the advantage of a ſtate, to have either public debts, or thoſe of individuals at a high intereſt; and I am perſuaded the doctor himſelf would not draw ſuch an inference from it, though ſome of his readers, I ſuſpect, will be apt to interpret it as an argument in favour of the high rate of intereſt. I will preſent the reader with a politico-arithmetical computation, drawn from the rate of intereſt, very different from the doctor's, but which proves to a demonſtration, that the low intereſt of money contributes eſſentially to lighten the burden of the national debts, or, in other words, enables the nation to bear ſuch a load as would overwhelm her if money were at an high intereſt. The great pledge for the ſecurity of the repayment of the national debt is the land of Great Britain;

tain; and it is an allowed maxim, confirmed by many facts for these hundred years past, that, as the interest of money has decreased, the value of lands is risen, nearly in the proportion of five years purchase for one per cent. diminution. Suppose money then at five per cent, and lands at twenty-five years purchase, the value of the great pledge will, in that case, be twenty-five times twenty-two millions, which will amount to five hundred and fifty millions. But if we suppose money at three per cent. the marketable value of the lands would be thirty-five years purchase, or seven hundred and seventy millions, that is, the pledge would be two hundred and twenty millions of pounds more valuable on the supposition of money at three per cent. than on that of money at five per cent. Another great pledge of security to the public creditors, is the annual stock of industry of the whole nation; and the more considerable this is, the more lightly the burden will be felt: but few things tend so much to increase industry as the low rate of interest; therefore the lessening that rate, till it be brought to a par with that of our commercial neighbours, ought to be a constant object of administration; and the beginning with Ireland will give a great facility in any operation of that kind in Great Britain†.

H   Another

---

† Mr. Pinto, greatly distinguished for his commercial and political knowledge, not only in England, but in Holland and France, has, in a late essay upon circulation, viewed the debts of Great Britain in a singular, but very erroneous light. According to him, the national debt is a mark of riches to Great Britain, as the low millions and a half that are paid annually to the public creditors, entering into a circulation in the state, so greatly augments the general wealth. But his reasoning upon the effects of circulation is altogether inconclusive, and has made him exaggerate any good effects that public debts may have had, without attending to their bad consequences.   Vid. page 12.

Another article in the proposed regulations is, That the additional taxes to be raised

he tells us; that four millions of taxes paid to the public creditors,
occasions fifteen or twenty millions in circulation; in another place
he affirms, that one million may produce twenty millions, and in
a third place, that three millions of rents may produce ten millions in
circulation. Those variations shew the uncertainty of the author, in
regard to the truth of his own principle, which will not bear the test
of analizing; for let us take his smallest estimate, that three millions
of rents give occasion to ten millions in circulation, in that proportion, twenty-six millions and a half, which is the amount of the land
rents and public annuities joined together, would occasion an annual
circulation in Great Britain of eighty-eight millions. But there is a-
nother active revenue in this state, of at least forty millions, which
produces the same effect in circulation as rents, consequently, in the
above proportion, this ought likewise to occasion a circulation of an
hundred and thirty-three millions, not to mention the king's revenue
or civil list, which ought to occasion a circulation of two millions six
hundred thousand pounds; and seven millions of taxes, which should
produce twenty-three millions in circulation. This would make a
sum total of annual circulation in Great Britain of two hundred and
forty-six millions; and if such is the sum at his smallest estimate, how
enormous would it be if taken at the highest proportion! Circulation
is but a general word, including all purchases and sales, or the uni-
versal expence of the people in their mutual traffic with each other;
and reckoning eight millions of people in Great Britain, two hundred
and forty-six millions of circulations would suppose an expence of near
thirty-one pounds per head, or, at six persons to a family, one hundred and eighty-three pounds for each family in Great Britain, when
it is probably not much above twelve pounds per head; and was
computed by Sir William Petty, an hundred years ago, but at five
pounds per head. Mr. Pinto's suppositions seem to be inconclusive
taken in another view; for if four millions of rents belonging to public creditors be of such importance to the state, five millions would be
still more so, and six millions still better; but I fancy few people will
believe that our circumstances would be improved by such an artificial
revenue, that could only be raised by an augmentation of taxes. I
must, however, do Mr. Pinto the justice to mention, that he himself
allows a *maximum*, which the public debts ought not to exceed,
though he places that *maximum* at a very great distance.

As the wealth and power of Great Britain are remarkably increased
within these sixty years, and it is likewise notorious, that our public
debts are more than tripled within the same space, I am afraid he has
suffered himself to be misled in believing the latter to be the cause of
the former. Other reasons, however, much more substantial than
those drawn from circulation, may be assigned why the nation has increased in power and opulence, notwithstanding the augmented burden
of the public debts. First, it may be allowed that those debts have
operated some good effects. All the money raised upon loans, during
our late foreign wars, has not been blown away in gun-powder;
much of it has been accumulated by those who have had transactions
with government, in consequence of which estates have been pur-
chased, lands improved, and many houses built upon new foundati-

building of ships of war, and to the maintaining and supporting a naval force in that
ifland. As a very important part of our dominion now lies beyond the Atlantic Ocean,
there is nothing Great Britain ought to give
more attention to at present than to the increafing her central maritime force. Inftead
of wafting great fums in colonizing defarts
in America, fhe ought to fpare no expence
in colonizing the fea coafts of Great Britain
and Ireland. Thefe two iflands together, and
not Great Britain alone, ought to be confidered as the *metropole*, or mother country of
all the colonies; therefore, when I mention
the increafing our central naval force as neceffary, I do not mean that it fhould all be
confined to the river Thames, or even to the
ports of Great Britain, The increafing naval fettlements upon all the coafts both of
Great Britain and Ireland, would be the moft
likely means of inducing many people to pur-
fue a feafaring life, and, confequently, of
augmenting our home naval ftrength. We
have hitherto, from a moft ill-judged jealoufy, feemed not to care how naked Ireland
was left of every thing that ferved to maintain dominion, while the North Americans
have been encouraged with all the fondnefs
of an indulgent parent to profecute fhip-
building, fifheries, and foreign commerce to
a very extenfive degree. Ireland, neverthelefs, has certainly a much more natural claim
to the prior attention of government; and
her intereft would have been much more
linked with that of Great Britain, if her maritime ports had been more numerous and
more

more confiderable. As the land force of
Ireland does not at prefent require any farther expence, the additional taxes propofed
could not be laid out more properly than in
eftablifhing a royal dock-yard in fome part
on the weftern or fouthern fhores of that
ifland. The local advantages of fuch an eftablifhment, in buildings, add confumption
of provifions, would redound to the country
where it was made; but the maritime ftrength
which it would raife, would as much apper-
tain to Great Britain as that of Portfmouth or
Plymouth; and the narfery of fhip-carpenters
and feamen, would as much ferve to advance
our commerce as if it were eftablifhed upon
the river Thames. The French and Spaniards have naval docks on the Atlantic
Ocean, as well as in the Mediterranean Sea;
but we who have now fo much concern with
the Atlantic, have yet no proper port upon
it. The chief royal dock-yard of France is
in the moft weftern port of that kingdom,
and in a province where the French language
is not generally underftood; yet, I believe,
few people acquainted at all with France, will
hefitate in determining, that the royal arfenal
is more advantageoufly fituated at Breft, than
it would be at the mouth of the Seine. An
armament fitted out in one of the weftern
ports of Ireland, for an expedition to the
Weftern or Southern Seas, might have the
advantage of three or four weeks over one
fitted out at Portfmouth for the fame defti-
nation, which would not only fhorten the
rifks at fea, but might be of great importance in regard to the lives of failors and
foldiers, and render the execution of the en-
terprize more certain, and lefs expenfive.
But

But instead of gaining an advantage of three or four weeks only, by fitting out on the western coast of Ireland, we might, on many occasions, gain a whole campaign, of which we had a disagreeable proof in the last war, in the armament fitted out against Louisburg; for, in all probability, had that armament been to set sail from the west of Ireland, it would have reached Cape Breton time enough to have reduced the place a year sooner, in consequence of which Canada might have been conquered, and the war happily terminated, without the expence of so many campaigns.

To sum up all, Ireland does not now stand in the same relation to Great Britain as formerly; therefore the period is arrived for a total change of political system in regard to that island. A skilful gardener is attentive to proportion the branches of his trees to the trunks that are to support them, and as Great Britain is daily expanding her branches to a wider extent over America, true policy would dictate to us the propriety of enlarging and strengthening the trunk that is to sustain those branches, by a communication of all commercial advantages to Ireland, and considering both islands but as one. Were we but studious to promote industry in Ireland, and in the distant provinces in Great Britain, we need be no more follicitous about the ballance of trade between the two islands, than about that between Southampton and the Isle of Wight, as the gain of either would be the national gain. Though many partial interests would be affected in both islands, by putting commerce upon an equal footing in each, yet the experience of the many ad-

vantages

vantages that have accrued to England and
Scotland by their mutual union, gives us a
most demonstrative proof that the general
national interest would be greatly promoted
by granting a freedom of trade to Ireland,
without any farther union of the two islands.
Were the number of trading vessels and sail-
ors in Ireland ten times greater than it now
is, Great Britain would have no cause of
apprehension from that, but rather matter of
rejoicing. Were Ireland, in all her ports,
to have naval docks, and numbers of ship-
carpenters; were her quantity of circulating
money to be doubled; were her lands to
produce four times as much as at present, and
her mines in general wrought to greater advantage, Great Britain, I say, would have
nothing to apprehend from all those circumstances, and from that accumulation of
power. That strength and riches would be
a strength and riches co-operating with ours.
The interests of both islands being put, as
they naturally ought to be, upon the same
level, the views of both would be the same;
and the greater their intercourse with each
other, the greater would be their happiness
and prosperity; but still the larger island,
having the advantage of the seat of empire,
would maintain the superiority of wealth
over the smaller. However valuable the balance of trade may be, yet to every state, the
strengthening the center of dominion ought
to be an object of much more importance.
But both these objects are now attainable by
Great Britain, in a most eminent degree, if
she will consent to throw away the jealousy
and rivalship of the trade of Ireland, and ad-
mit that island to an equal participation of
advantages

advantages wirh herfelf, in every poinc rela-
tive to foreign commerce. If we regard fo-
lidity and duration, the higher we wifh to
raife the pyramid, the broader we ought to
make the bafe.

THE END.

www.ingramcontent.com/pod-product-compliance
Lightning Source LLC
Chambersburg PA
CBHW021521090426
42739CB00007B/720